Original title:
Frosted Mornings and Frozen Skies

Copyright © 2024 Creative Arts Management OÜ
All rights reserved.

Author: Elliot Harrison
ISBN HARDBACK: 978-9916-94-612-1
ISBN PAPERBACK: 978-9916-94-613-8

Morning Mist and Glinting Crystals

The morning breeze is quite a tease,
As snowflakes dance and twirl like bees.
I slip and slide, it's quite a ride,
My dignity shatters in the freeze aside.

Those glinting bits, they catch my eye,
A crow on the fence gives me a sly.
I swear I hear it chuckle with glee,
As I flail around like a clumsy bee.

Winter Whispers from the North

Oh, the whispers tell me to dress up warm,
But my socks come from last Halloween's swarm!
I stumble outside, oh what a sight,
Wearing plaid pants that don't quite fit right.

The postman slides past, grinning wide,
While I cautiously tiptoe, trying to glide.
A snowball flies out, I duck and dive,
Turns out I'm just a snowman's jive!

Vows in the Snow

I promised to shovel, in the fluff so white,
But the snow is a monster, it gives me a fright.
I grab the shovel, feeling so bold,
It laughs and whispers, 'You're just getting old!'

Around the house, I trip and flip,
Each vow I made gives a little slip.
Who knew that snow could be such a foe?
My love for winter is starting to slow!

The Palette of Dim Light and Ice

The sunrise peeks with colors so neat,
While I'm stuck blending in with my feet.
My toes feel numb, my nose, a bright red,
Guess the ice wasn't ready for me to tread!

With colors bright, the sky does jest,
But I'm still in pajamas, trying my best.
A cat then leaps onto my hat,
And suddenly, winter's not so flat.

A Tapestry of Shimmering White

Snowflakes tumble, oh what a sight,
Landing in my hair, what a fright!
I slip and slide, a graceful turn,
Chasing after snowmen, I crash and learn.

Cherubs laugh from rooftops high,
While I'm wedged in a snowdrift, oh my!
Snowball fights become quite the game,
Till someone yells, 'Hey! You've got no aim!'

When Wonder Meets a Wintry Canvas

Sledding down hills at breakneck speed,
Screams of joy, oh the thrill we plead!
Hot cocoa waits with marshmallow fluff,
As we paint our cheeks, just a bit too rough.

Snowmen smile with buttons askew,
Their crooked hats: a sight quite askew!
We build them tall, then watch them fall,
I swear I heard one ask, 'Is this my all?'

Whispers of an Icy Dawn

Morning sparkles, light on the ground,
I slip on ice, oh what a sound!
My dog takes off, chasing after a crow,
While I dive face-first into soft, white snow.

Birds chirp loudly, 'What's taking so long?'
As I laugh, my pants sing a cold, wet song!
A snow angel made with flailing limbs,
While the sun just giggles and slowly skims.

Crystals on Windowpanes

Morning stretches with sparkly dreams,
Frost dances across the windows with schemes.
I grab a warm mug, take a big sip,
Only to spill it, oh what a drip!

Nature's art is finely drawn,
While I frolic in fluff, like a lion at dawn.
Chasing sunlight, I slip and glide,
Wishing for grace, but finding my pride!

Butterscotch Skies and Frigid Air

In the frosty light of day,
Squirrels dance in wild ballet,
They slip and slide, oh what a show,
While we sip cocoa nice and slow.

Chasing ice with dreamy ease,
I stumbled once, then twice, then wheeze!
My nose is red, not from the sun,
But from the cold; oh, what fun!

The Lullaby of Whispering Winds

The wind sings soft a playful tune,
As snowflakes swirl 'neath the bright moon,
Chasing my hat with quite the flair,
It skips away, oh, what a scare!

Ice skates croon on frozen lakes,
I do a twirl, but my balance breaks,
I tumble down with a shocked surprise,
And giggles pierce the chilly skies.

Haikus Beneath the Ice

Chill tickles my toes,
Penguins waddle and they pose,
Ice cream's in the air!

Snowmen wear my hat,
Grinning wide, imagine that,
Did he just tip me?

Snowballs fly like dreams,
Laughter bursts at the seams,
Winter's silly schemes.

Melodies of the Morning Frost

Puffing clouds of breath, we sing,
As icicles jingle and swing,
The cat leaps out just to prance,
But lands in snow—it's quite the dance!

Chasing rafts of glistening white,
My socks are soaked, but what a sight!
With every slide and tiny spill,
We laugh and shout, oh what a thrill!

Tapestry of Icy Dreams

In a land where penguins wear shoes,
The sun's gotten lost, don't know what to choose.
Snowflakes dance wildly, they twist and they twirl,
Even the frost tries to give winter a whirl.

The trees wear their coats, all buttoned up tight,
Squirrels debate if they should take a flight.
The rivers are snoring, all frozen in place,
While snowmen conspire with a snowball face.

Secrets Hidden Beneath the Chill

Beneath the white cover, a secret lies low,
A family of mice throws a mid-winter show.
With cheese for confetti and snow for the stage,
They squeak out a tune that sparks winter's rage.

Frosty the snowman got trapped in a bind,
Waving his twig arms; he's lost all his mind.
"Hey buddy! Just breathe! You're all made of snow!"
But someone misplaced his carrot, oh no!

Lament of the Shivering Boughs

With a clatter and clink, the branches complain,
The wind's got a cold chill, it's driving them insane.
They chatter their leaves, in a whispering spree,
"Stop blowing so hard, you're still ten degrees!"

The owls in their coats are having a laugh,
Counting the icicles like their own photograph.
While rabbits in scarves hop about with glee,
Eating their carrots, just as bold as can be.

Time in a Crystal Ball

In a globe full of chill and a giggle or two,
A wizard stares sharply at winter's grand view.
"I see you in mittens, oh hear the snicker,
The ice will be melting, but first take a picture!"

The months march along, all frosty and bright,
With marshmallow clouds in a sugary white.
Each tick of the clock is a snowflake's prank,
Let's laugh 'til we slide down a powdery bank!

A Tundra's Quiet Story

In a land where the cold likes to play,
The snowmen wear hats, come what may.
They stand with their arms all akimbo,
While penguins slide by, yelling, "Bingo!"

A polar bear dances, quite out of step,
With a penguin who thinks he's a rep.
They twirl and they whirl, what a sight!
As the sun peeks in, making everything bright.

Icicles hang from every eave,
Shiny and sharp, like tricks up their sleeve.
But when the dog jumps in the snow,
He finds that the ground is quite a show!

So, gather around, for the tales will unfold,
Of a tundra where laughter is weathered and bold.
With snowflakes that giggle and giggles that freeze,
In this chilly arena, no one's at ease.

Enigma of Chill and Light

As dawn breaks in hues of pastel delight,
Squirrels shuffle, all bundled up tight.
They chatter and giggle, what's this they spied?
A snowball brigade led by a rabbit so spry!

A snow angel lands, looking rather grand,
But wait! Who's that? Oh, it's just Timmy's hand.
He jumps in surprise at his own fluff-filled flight,
While the geese honk in humor, oh what a sight!

The sun beams down, casting shadows that prance,
As winter-time friends join in a dance.
With mittens that slip and scarves that entwine,
They tumble and roll, in a flurry divine.

So let's lift our mugs with frothy hot cheer,
To the mischief of winter we hold so dear.
With laughter that echoes through crisp, frosty air,
This chill comes alive, it's a whimsical affair!

Celestial Veils in Twilight

With a wink, the sun is late,
It slipped on ice, what a fate!
The clouds are dressed in silly styles,
Dancing lightly, wearing smiles.

A snowman plays a trumpet tune,
While squirrels hold a winter boon.
The trees are giggling in their coats,
As penguins glide on skates like boats.

The icicles are sharp and bright,
But they twinkle with sheer delight.
Snowflakes send a flurry of cheer,
As hot cocoa warms the cold, oh dear!

In this world where whimsy reigns,
Every snowball fight leaves stains.
So laugh and play through chilly climes,
For winter's just one big, funny rhyme.

Portrait of a Blue Haze

The sky wore a blanket, oh so chilly,
Like grandma's quilt, warm yet silly.
Birds are wearing knitted caps,
Flying fast in joyous laps.

The moon is stuck, oh what a plight,
In the pancake clouds, a fluffy sight.
As snowmen scheme with carrots for noses,
What chaos lies beneath the poses!

Each puff of breath is a work of art,
Like frosted doodles from the heart.
The sun peeks out, gives a goofy grin,
While the frost on trees starts to win.

Slippers on paws, the raccoons prance,
Inviting all for a winter dance.
In the delightful, icy maze,
We lose ourselves in this blue haze.

Glistening Paths of Solitude

In solitude, the snowflakes whirl,
Spinning dreams in a frozen twirl.
Bunnies dashing without a care,
While sipping cocoa in the air.

Each glistening path is a silly sign,
Leading to where the giggles align.
Uplifted spirits in the frosty night,
As snowmen chuckle in pure delight.

Comets whizzing passed the trees,
Rabbits tugging their mittens with ease.
A whimsical dance, all nature plays,
On hidden trails where laughter stays.

So bundle up for this icy spree,
Where every step's a chance to be free.
In the hush of snow, embrace with glee,
These paths of joy, it's meant to be!

Scribe of the Snowy Hours

A scribe of snowflakes, quick and sly,
Writes secrets from the frosty sky.
The ink is cold, a liquid freeze,
Tickling noses in a winter breeze.

Each letter falls with a giggling thud,
While kittens slide in the frosty mud.
Chasing tails through mounds so grand,
Building castles in a winter land.

With every blink, the world feels bright,
Even puddles take on delight.
The sun can't help but join the fun,
While shadows play, what a run!

So let this chill be a playful friend,
With jokes and laughter that never end.
In these snowy hours, we find a way,
To savor joy in a frosty play.

Phantom Colors in the Gloaming

In the dawn, the sun looks shy,
Painting clouds with a jelly pie.
The squirrels wear hats, a silly sight,
As they dance around, oh what a delight!

A igloo stand, with a laugh so loud,
Penguins in suits, all proudly bowed.
A snowman's nose, it's made of cheese,
Wobbling around, as wobbly as you please!

Hot cocoa flows like a flowing stream,
With marshmallow islands that surely gleam.
But watch your step, it's slippery here,
Or you might just end up eating a deer!

So let's embrace this wacky chill,
With giggles, snowballs, and time to kill.
The world is bright in its frosted dress,
Amidst all the laughs, we find happiness!

The Edge of Everywhere Frozen

On the brink of the world, it all feels odd,
A snowman's dancing, he thinks he's God.
With carrot feet and a lopsided grin,
It's hard to tell where the fun begins!

Puffy clouds like whipped cream float,
While kids on sleds go zooming, remote.
But watch out for cats, they're plotting a strike,
Chasing snowflakes like they're on a bike!

Frost has made the trees look bizarre,
With branches like fingers reaching far.
But snow-chickens cluck, and they all agree,
Winter's a circus, come join the spree!

So laugh at the cold, let your breath puff steam,
Join in the craziness, follow your dream.
For at the edge, where everything's froze,
There's magic and giggles like nobody knows!

A Tapestry of Snowbound Memories

A patchwork quilt of white and blue,
The ground is fuzzy, a giant's shoe.
The laughter echoes, playful and bright,
As sleds crash down—oh, what a sight!

Snowflakes tickle like a feathered kiss,
While penguins skate in perfect bliss.
A scarecrow named Fred is having a show,
His dance is silly, it steals the snow!

Hot cocoa swirls in a giant cup,
While marshmallow fluffs bounce all the way up.
Happy snow bunnies hopping all around,
Each leap brings laughter, a joyful sound!

So gather 'round, let stories unfold,
In crazy winter, the best tales are told.
We weave our laughter 'neath the chilly beam,
As we create a tapestry, frosted with dream!

Beneath the Lunar Ice

Under the moon, it's a slippery bash,
Jack Frost is hosting a wild, snowy clash.
With snowmen waltzing and penguins on skates,
They send frosty invitations to all the great mates!

Icicles chime like bells on a spree,
While snowballs target the unsuspecting bee.
The owls have gathered, they plot and they scheme,
Laughing and hooting, it's quite the meme!

Frostbite jokes fly like stars in the night,
As rabbits in scarves hop about all light.
Beware of the snowmen; they're up to no good,
With carrots in hand, they're misunderstood!

So raise a toast with your frosty mug high,
Join the laughter beneath painted skies.
For in this winter wonder, the fun never dies,
As we dance and discover beneath lunar ice!

Under a Blanket of Sparkling Quiet

Wrapped in white, I can't find my toes,
But I hear the crunch wherever I go.
I slip and slide, a clumsy ballet,
Like a penguin trying to escape the gray.

Neighbors peek out, eyes wide in surprise,
As I tumble down, 'neath the cloud-filled skies.
Laughter erupts from the frosty ground,
In this winter wonderland, joy can be found.

Snowflakes dancing, a whimsical show,
I might not have grip, but I'll give it a go.
Hot cocoa spills everywhere in my dash,
But the taste of the season? A frosty splash!

So here I am, under blankets of cheer,
With giggles and grace, I'll push aside fear.
In sparkling stillness, I revel and sway,
Embracing the chaos in a snowball play.

Frost-kissed Haze of Morning's Embrace

The grass is frozen, a canvas of white,
And my nose is red; oh what a sight!
I start off bright, a bundle of glee,
But watch me slip, oh woe is me!

I grab my shovel, thinking I'm tough,
But that snow's like a prankster, it's pretty rough.
With each swing and thrust, I'm out of control,
Waging a battle with a frosty patrol.

Sipping hot tea while wrapped like a burrito,
My cat gives me looks like I'm quite the weirdo.
Yet outside is a glitter, a sparkling tease,
Winter's silly dance puts my mind at ease.

As I trip through the yard, intrepid and brave,
I laugh at the freeze; oh how I misbehave!
In this chilly embrace, I'm a marvel to see,
A snow-covered jester, just winter and me!

Ethereal Glimmers in Chilled Air

Morning creeps in, all glimmer and shine,
With icicles hanging, it's quite the design.
I step out ready, with boots on my feet,
But my hat flies away, well isn't that sweet?

The trees look like candles, all draped in their white,
While squirrels hoard acorns, prepared for a fight.
They dart in and out, a frosty charade,
As I chase after warmth, my plans start to fade.

With cheeks that are rosy, a glow that won't quit,
I make snow angels; good luck with that fit!
The laughter erupts with each tumble and spin,
Creating a tapestry of wintery grin.

And as the day fades, with a dip of the sun,
I head for the warmth, but oh what a run!
In ethereal moments, I relish my fun,
Even frozen, there's joy in this frosty pun!

The Stillness That Icy Dawn Brings

A hush falls around, like a fluffy white hug,
While I shuffle out, giving winter a tug.
The air crackles crisp, a comic delight,
As snowmen are built like quirky old sights.

Each breath is a puff of freezing white air,
And my cheeks feel like apples, so rosy and rare.
With cold toes a-dancing, I holler and scream,
As I slip on a patch, oh! This isn't a dream!

The sun peeks out like a mischievous guy,
And I squint at the sparkle; oh my, oh my!
The shadows are long, like a tall tale of fright,
Yet in this frozen state, I find pure delight.

So here's to the mornings where laughter is free,
In a world made of glimmers, just winter and me.
The stillness is broken with jokes in the air,
As icicles chime like a winter affair!

Candles of Ice and Sunny Rays

Chilly air nips at our toes,
As we slip on socks like furry foes.
Snowmen giggle, wearing hats so wide,
While penguins slide with arctic pride.

The sun peeks out, a stealthy spy,
Warming cheeks as we wave goodbye.
Hot cocoa spills, a marshmallow dive,
Laughter erupts, we're more than alive!

Glimmering Traces on an Amethyst Canvas

Crystals sparkle on the ground,
Boots make crunches, what a sound!
A snowflake lands upon my nose,
And tickles me, oh how it goes!

Snowball fights, oh such delight,
Dodging flurries left and right.
We build a fort, a snowy lair,
Where ice dragons loom in frosty air!

A Dance of Light Over Crystalline Fields

The sun winks at frozen trees,
As squirrels chatter, making cheese.
While snowflakes twirl in a dizzying spree,
I chase them barefoot, wild and free!

Icicles dangle like glistening teeth,
As winter's breath dances beneath.
We twirl and whirl in the chilly breeze,
Laughing so hard, we spill our freeze!

Still Waters Under a Shimmering Sky

Reflections glimmer where ducks do glide,
They quack in chorus, what a ride!
We pirouette on the icy sheet,
With grins so wide, we can't be beat.

But oops! Down goes, oh what a sight,
My flailing arms, a comical flight!
The ducks all quack, a raucous cheer,
As I laugh and tumble, with festive cheer!

Radiant Animals Leave Their Trace

In the crisp air, bunnies hop high,
Chasing each other, oh me, oh my!
Squirrels in sweaters, looking quite bold,
Dancing on branches, all covered in gold.

Foxes in boots, what a sight to behold,
Sliding on ice, or so they are told.
With tails like scarves, swish and sway,
Winter's little critters, come out to play.

Deer with goggles, so stylish and chic,
Tiptoe through snow, with a playful squeak.
A parade of fun under glimmer and chill,
Nature's own jesters, it gives us a thrill.

Laughs in the air, what a ruckus they make,
Chasing their shadows, a joyful mistake.
In this winter wonderland, we all take a chance,
To giggle and frolic, in this snowy dance.

Glacial Hearts that Beat Slow

In the quiet hours, when the world feels still,
A penguin slides down a frosty hill.
Waddling with flair, he gives it a go,
Crashes abound, but it's all part of the show.

Snowflakes twirl, landing right on his hat,
A snowman chuckles, 'You look like a cat!'
He stands there proud, with a carrot for a nose,
Even in the chill, it's laughter that grows.

Chilly little hearts, beating just so,
Trying to dance in a blizzard's flow.
With iced cocoa sips, they giggle and grin,
In this frozen wonderland, joy spills from within.

Each frosty moment feels oddly profound,
While pine trees shake off their snow with a sound.
Together they share a hearty delight,
In this frigid affair, everything's bright!

Flights under Frostbound Dreams

High in the sky, where the cold winds whistle,
A flock of birds, drawing tales with a crystal.
Wings frosted white, like a dragon's breath,
Soaring together, defying the depth.

They giggle and squeak, in the chill of the air,
Making snow angels without a care.
Frosty tomfoolery, their laughter erupts,
As they tumble and twirl, in frosty big jumps.

Each landing a giggle, each take-off a cheer,
They gather in groups, shedding all fear.
In snowflake ballet, they twirl and they spin,
In the realm of the chilly, their fun shall begin.

With frozen beaks, they chirp out a rhyme,
Winter's bright jesters, just having a time.
Under the boughs of the trees dressed in white,
They create a soft magic on a whimsical flight.

Lanterns Shining Through the Cold

A lantern's glow in the frosted night,
Dances with shadows, oh what a sight!
Bubbling with laughter, a playful delight,
As the world turns sparkly, beneath silver light.

Snowflakes twinkle, like stars on the ground,
In the chill of the evening, cheer is all around.
A snowflake bash, with a jolly old tune,
Laughter erupts, with the rise of the moon.

Hot cocoa swirls, with marshmallows afloat,
As friends gather 'round, in their mittens they gloat.
Swapping funny tales by the warmth of the glow,
Creating memories in the chilly tableau.

With lanterns aglow, every heart feels light,
In the laughter and joy, we find our delight.
Wrapped in dear moments, we cherish the cold,
In the warmth of our laughter, together we're bold.

Ephemeral Embers of Light

In the morning's chill, a frosty bite,
Everyone's shivering, it gives such a fright.
Snowmen are grinning, with carrots in tow,
Let's build them a hat, a real winter show!

Hot chocolate's brewing, it's a funny delight,
Marshmallows dive in, taking a bite.
The cat on the windowsill, cozy and stout,
Pawing at snowflakes, what's that all about?

Sledding down hills like it's a grand race,
With cheeks all aglow, we embrace the cold face.
But one silly slip, I tumble and roll,
Laughter erupts, oh, what a cold hole!

So grab your mittens, come join in the fun,
Chasing each snowflake 'til the day is done.
In this wintry wonder, we cherish and jest,
Finding joy in the cold, it's simply the best!

The Frosty Canvas Unfolds

Morning breaks gently, in blankets of white,
Painting the rooftops, what a whimsical sight!
Birds puff their feathers, with beaks all aglow,
Guess they forgot where they left their warm show!

Children bundled up, like marshmallows tight,
Launching snowballs in an epic snow fight.
Giggles and laughter, get lost in the flurry,
Quick dodge to the left, what a funny hurry!

A snowman is wobbly, with eyes made of coal,
He waves as we pass, with a snow-laden pole.
We cheer for his strength, he stands proud and round,
Till a dog comes along, and he's knocked to the ground!

But oh, how we giggle, we wipe frozen tears,
Sharing in moments that brighten cold years.
Sprinkling our joy, like snowflakes that fly,
Filling each day with a chuckle and sigh!

Glistening Tales of December

In the heart of December, joy leaps and bounds,
With snowflakes that twirl, making soft, funny sounds.
Tiptoeing over, the ice makes a crack,
One slip, and I'm down! Hey, don't turn your back!

The trees wear white dresses, a formal affair,
While squirrels in mittens scurry everywhere.
They're hoarding their treasures, oh such a sight,
Look at them giggle, chasing snow in delight!

A penguin parade at our local mall,
They slide and they waddle, oh isn't life small?
With laughter erupting at each snowy leap,
These tales of December, so funny and deep!

So gather your friends, let's dance in the cold,
With stories of winters that never get old.
Through laughter and snow, and the joy that we bring,
We'll twirl through the frost, like a happy, bright spring!

A Dance of Cold and Light

A shiver and shake in the morning's embrace,
The world wears a smile, like a big snowy face.
The sun tries to shine, through branches so sleek,
But it slips on the ice and gets cold on the cheek!

Children are slipping, a frosty ballet,
Waltzing on sidewalks, oh what a display!
Each giggle and tumble, a merry old sight,
Winter's just laughing, what a frosty delight!

Grandma's baking cookies, her secret's a blast,
With flour on her nose, oh my, what a cast!
Each taste is like magic, there's giggles galore,
And the cat? He's wearing our favorite scarf's core!

So come join our party, with snowballs in hand,
Let's dance with the snowflakes, it's simply well-planned.

In this waltz of the chilly, with laughter so bright,
We'll cherish these moments, all day, every night!

Heartbeat of the Slumbering Fields

The cows wear coats, it's quite a sight,
They moo through flurries, pure delight.
A snowman dances, or so it seems,
In plaid pajamas, lost in dreams.

The tractors slide, they twist and turn,
Like a dance-off gone wrong, all lessons unlearned.
Fields of white with cow tracks galore,
As laughter echoes, we all want more.

Chickens in boots, they strut with pride,
Leaving tiny prints, they take it in stride.
The harvest moon chuckles from above,
As winter plays, twirling with love.

So raise a mug, toast to the chill,
For these silly moments, oh, what a thrill!
In slumbering fields, where laughter rings,
We find the joy that winter brings.

Winter's Ethereal Lament

The trees wear icing, like cakes on a stand,
With branches that sparkle, they wave their hand.
But squirrels in coats, they plot and they scheme,
To steal those icicles, or so it would seem.

Snowflakes are teasing, they whiz and they race,
A flurry of pranks in this cold, frosty place.
The frozen pond laughs, but beware the fall,
As ice-dancing penguins prepare for their call.

The sun peeks out for a watchful delight,
While snowmen impersonate folks in the night.
They wobble and giggle, then tumble around,
With noses of carrots, they roll on the ground.

So let the air spark with laughter and fun,
In this wintery world, joy has just begun!
With snowball fights and ice cream cone dreams,
Let's savor the winter and its silly themes.

Scattered Stars on a Gelid Canvas

The night wears a blanket of shimmering chill,
While snowflakes sprinkle with whimsical thrill.
Bunnies in scarves hop with a cheer,
Giggling at shadows, not a worry or fear.

The moon winks down, a hearty delight,
Casting strange shapes in the shimmering night.
A reindeer in shades doing boogie-woogie,
With a jolly ol' grin, just a little bit goofy.

Icicles hang like glistening spears,
While muffled laughter erupts through the tears.
Frosty the Snowman, with a top hat askew,
Marches with flair, oh, how he does crew!

Under the stars, where the fun never ends,
We gather around, all the frosty, cold friends.
In this frozen wonder, we dance and we play,
Laughing and singing, in snowy ballet.

The Muffled Echoes of Twilight

As shadows stretch long, a hush fills the air,
While snowflakes whisper secrets with flair.
The owls hold a meeting about who's the best,
Sipping hot cocoa, they plot their next jest.

Beneath frosty branches, a choir of mice,
Sing off-key carols, oh, that's quite nice!
With tiny red mittens, they're dressed to impress,
In a world made of magic, what a grand mess!

The stars start to giggle, it's time for a game,
Chasing each other, they don't feel the shame.
While the moon rolls its eyes, just a light-hearted tease,
It offers a wink to the playful breeze.

So here's to the twilight, a time quite absurd,
Where frozen fun thrives and silliness stirred.
In this snowy shindig, we'll dance through the night,
Wrapped in soft laughter, till the morning light.

The Hush Before Dawn's Golden Hour

In the kitchen, the kettle sings,
While the cat takes flight on invisible wings.
The toast is doing a little dance,
As I try to give the coffee a chance.

Outside, the world wears a glimmering coat,
The squirrel forgot his secret note.
He hops and skips, looking quite absurd,
Chasing his tail like a fluffy nerd.

The sun peeks out, a cheeky tease,
Warmth arriving like jokes at a sneeze.
Mist hitches a ride on a passing car,
Waving goodbye to the night's bizarre.

And just like that, the day's begun,
Tripping over laughter, oh what fun!
With whispers of ice and giggles in tow,
Who knew the dawn could steal the show?

Enchanted by the Chill of New Beginnings

The mailbox stands like a frozen knight,
Holding letters that flutter in pure delight.
I swipe at the reeds, with a wing and a grin,
Befriending the frosty air, let the games begin!

My fingers turn into popsicles, bright,
As I brace for adventure with all of my might.
The ground crunches under my silly boots,
Each step a symphony, oh how it hoots!

The dog dashes off on a frolicsome spree,
Chasing the ice-cream truck, maybe a bee?
He slips on a patch, end over tail,
Turning the morning into a comedy tale!

With snowflakes laughing like silly little sprites,
Happiness drips from the world's frosty heights.
As daybreak unfolds with a wink and a spark,
Magic and mayhem reign in the park!

Luminous Frost on Sleeping Trees

Trees dressed in diamonds, so bold and bright,
Stand guard like soldiers in the morning light.
But one little branch just sneezed with flair,
Sending a shower of glitter through the air.

A bird, a chatterbox, fluffs up with zest,
Proclaiming a radio show, ready to jest.
He squawks about winter like it's a new craze,
While frosty leaves giggle in shimmering praise.

Nearby a snowman, all chubby and round,
Has a carrot that's more of a frown than a crown.
He tried for a wink, but his eyes did stare,
Looking quite puzzled, like he's stuck mid-air.

And as I sip on my steaming mug,
The world is a canvas with a cozy hug.
With laughter wrapped in the morning's embrace,
Every twinkle and whisper feels like a race!

Echoes of Daylight's Gentle Arrival

The sun rolls out of bed, yawning wide,
Stretching lazy beams through the grass outside.
Birds are singing, but one hits a wrong note,
Laughing at noon while he tunes up his coat.

A rabbit, in pajamas, hops on the scene,
Spinning in circles, oh what a routine!
With frost in his whiskers and mischief in mind,
He dances through gardens, one of a kind.

The sky wears a blanket, stitched in light blue,
While clouds make shapes like a fuzzy old shoe.
Oh! There's a snowflake, trying to stay cool,
But it pirouettes down, looking like a fool.

As laughter bounces through the crisp morning air,
And giggles glide by without a care,
The day gets brighter, and we all let it be,
In this whimsical world, oh what joy to see!

Canvas of Frozen Fantasies

At dawn, the world is dressed in white,
Squirrels slip and slide, what a silly sight!
Snowflakes dance down with a giggly flair,
Even the trees wear a chilly stare.

A penguin passed by, stealing my hat,
He wobbled and laughed, just imagine that!
In boots two sizes too big, I stride,
Landing face-first, my dignity died.

Hot cocoa spills on my brand new coat,
I guess marshmallows too, can't emote!
The sun peeks out, it does a jig,
While I struggle to move, oh it's big!

Around me, icicles dangle like teeth,
Reminding me this is no place for a wreath!
Each breath becomes puffs of cloudy air,
Who knew winter could be such a dare!

Echoes of the Unseen

In shadows, critters leap and glide,
While I try to shuffle, yet I slide!
Snowmen gossip with carrot noses high,
Planning their takeover, oh my, oh my!

A yeti took selfies with my old chair,
I caught him grinning, imagine that stare!
My old dog barks at all the lost socks,
Who knew winter was filled with such shocks?

Wind chimes ring out, singing silly tunes,
While I trip over my snowshoe balloons!
Every step's a venture of comedic flair,
Oh winter, you dare with frosty despair!

I built a snow fort like a brave little knight,
Until I was pelted; oh, what a sight!
Snowballs fly faster than the mind can think,
Here I am, trapped under ice with a wink!

Radiance of Winter's Kiss

The morning beams shine with a frosty grin,
As I make my way with a wild spin!
Snow piles up like fluffy cotton candy,
Who needs a gym? This is quite dandy!

My nose is red, like Rudolph's bright glow,
Chasing my hat that's caught in the flow!
Snowflakes landing on dogs with a thunk,
"Catch me if you can!" they merrily junk!

Skating on ponds like a pro gone rogue,
With graceful trips, I looked like a toad!
Even the crows laugh, making it known,
Winter's a stage, where laughs have grown!

At dusk, the stars twinkle like a joke,
Around the fire, warmth, we invoke!
Who knew the cold could bring such delight?
With comedic tales that last through the night!

Days Wrapped in Silver

Blankets of snow hug the ground so tight,
While I stomp about, a comical sight!
Beneath frosty pines, I find a lost shoe,
And mutter aloud, "Now, what's a girl to do?"

Laser-guided goggles for snowball fights,
Yet still, I'm hit by my own frozen sights!
A snow angel whispers, "You need some grace!"
I giggle and flop, "Let me give it a chase."

Snowdrifts pile high, like mounds of whipped cream,
As my car stubbornly refuses to beam!
With shovels like swords, we battle the frost,
But the laughter we share will never be lost!

At twilight we gather, the hot cocoa flows,
Each sip brings warmth as the merriment grows!
So here's to the winter with its giddy parade,
Where fun takes the stage, and troubles do fade!

A Canvas of Whispered Blues

The world wrapped tight in chilly wraps,
Socks on hands, our funny mishaps.
Penguins prance on icy grounds,
In woolly sweaters, laughter abounds.

Snowflakes giggle, dainty and light,
They tickle noses in morning's bite.
Hot cocoa rivers, marshmallow boats,
Sipping with friends, while winter gloats.

Birds wear boots, or so it seems,
Flapping their wings, as if in dreams.
Snowmen strut, with carrot dreams,
While we all ponder winter memes.

In frosted fields, the snowflakes tease,
Tickling toes, with a chilly breeze.
Nature laughs with a sparkling grin,
As we dance on ice, wearing winter's skin.

Nature's Silent Elegy

In blankets white, the world is still,
Chasing snowballs gives quite a thrill.
Sleds rush down with squeals and cheers,
Till crashes bring about snowy tears.

Icicles dangle, sharp as a knife,
Beware, they might end your sledding life!
Bunny hops through the glowing drifts,
In search of snacks, he surely whiffs.

The trees wear crowns of snowy lace,
And squirrels plot their winter race.
Nutty conspiracies fill the air,
While branches sway without a care.

Chatter and laughter mix with the chill,
As we tumble, roll, and embrace the thrill.
Though winter may seem a frosty chore,
It's a playground just waiting to explore!

Frozen Hues Beneath Expanding Skies

Beneath the clouds, a canvas wide,
Painted with jokes that tickle inside.
Snowflakes fall like little clowns,
Dancing down to quit the frowns.

Ghostly shadows, we'd swear they move,
Sledders glide with a comical groove.
The ice rink's a no-slip zone,
With wobbly friends who've lost their throne.

Snowball fights ignite friendly wars,
As laughter echoes off of doors.
Hot drinks in hands, the winter's cheer,
With silly warmth, we'll persevere.

So take a leap, let joys collide,
In winter's laughter, there's love inside.
As frozen hues paint all we see,
With chuckles that are wild and free.

The Breath of a Winter's Sun

The sun peeks shy 'neath frosty veils,
While we sip on warm, sweet ales.
Jackets zipped, we shuffle along,
In a world where the snowmen play strong.

The air is crisp, but jokes are warm,
As puns swirl in a wintery storm.
Noses red like ripe tomatoes,
Slip and slide, but we know the closes.

Snowflakes tumble and twist with glee,
A flurry of joy, just wait and see!
With snowshoes on, we make our mark,
Finding fun beneath the stark.

In the glimmering light, we'll find our way,
Bouncing in joy, come what may.
With each step, our spirits run,
Riding winter's wave, oh what fun!

The Poetry of Slumbering Trees

Trees in blankets soft and white,
Snoring softly, what a sight!
Bark wrapped tight, they dream of sun,
While branches chat about the fun.

Squirrels sneak, with acorn treats,
But branches roll their sleepy beats.
Pine-cones giggle, wobbling around,
Their winter tales are quite profound.

Birds in coats of fluff and cheer,
Whisper secrets, too cold to hear.
But oh! The trees, in lazy ways,
Will snooze through all those winter days.

Let's all take naps, and hold our tea,
Become like trees in slumber, whee!
With frosty dreams and silly thoughts,
A cozy world is what we've got!

Chasing Shadows in the Chill

Shadows skip like children play,
Dancing though it's bleak and gray.
Snowflakes tumble, oh so sly,
"Catch me, catch me!" as they fly.

Winter boots stomp on the ground,
Every step a squeaky sound.
Slipping, sliding, what a thrill,
Chasing shadows up a hill.

Frosty noses, cheeks all red,
Puppies prance, their joy widespread.
Yet every chase leads to a fall,
With muffled giggles heard by all.

So grab a friend, let's take a race,
Through the chill, we'll set the pace.
Forget the frost; let's laugh and play,
Who cares if we freeze the day away?

Reflections in the Morning Mist

In the mist, reflections gleam,
Looking lost, like half a dream.
A bird's shadow makes me frown,
"What is that, a floating crown?"

Rabbits hopping, full of glee,
Waving tails, just like a spree.
I swear I saw a snowman grin,
Wishing he had legs to spin.

Puddles freeze, a mirror's prank,
A sheen of ice—how quaint, how dank!
I stumble here, and teeter there,
Is that a winking polar bear?

But through the haze, I find a cheer,
Chasing laughter, bright and clear.
So let's embrace this frosty gust,
With silly antics, that's a must!

NFTs of Winter Archetypes

In the digital realm, winter reigns,
Trading snowflakes like silly chains.
A snowman glows, a pixel spark,
His carrot nose, oh what a lark!

Penguins swap their dance moves too,
"Check my NFT, it's very new!"
A frosty fractal in cool shades,
Blockchain snow where fun cascades.

Icicle NFTs, sharp and bright,
Owning one feels oddly right.
Balloons of winter float and sway,
In this art, we laugh and play.

So click and mint, come join the fun,
Each frosty asset better run!
In frozen markets, let's conspire,
For winter's humor won't expire!

Glacial Serenade at Daybreak

The sun peeks out, a shy young sprite,
Wrapped in blankets, it's quite a sight.
Chattering teeth join the morning song,
As winter's breath plays all day long.

Snowflakes dance in an icy ballet,
While socks mismatched come out to play.
Icicles hang like nature's teeth,
Giggles echo as we try to breathe.

Breakfast pancakes have turned to stone,
The dog's shiny coat is a frozen cone.
Sipping cocoa, the steam does rise,
Creating mustaches that tease our eyes.

As snowballs fly in a wild spree,
I slip and slide—oh, look at me!
Winter's charm, like a jolly prank,
Keeps us laughing as our cheeks turn pink.

When the World Wears White

Waking up to a glittery mess,
The cat's stuck in a snow-covered dress.
Boots on feet, we leap and glide,
Overcoming slips with some winter pride.

Parks are filled with frosty cheer,
Where snowmen wobble, their eyes sincere.
Each carrot nose is a noble wish,
An epic face with a fruity dish.

Hats too big just bobble around,
While snowflakes swoop like fairies unbound.
A shoveling shuffle turns into a dance,
Who knew cold could give us this chance?

Some let snowball fights begin,
Dodging and ducking as laughter spins.
With footprints trailing like tiny clues,
We wrap up warmth in this snowy snooze.

Glistening Echoes of a Quiet Awakening

The world's a canvas, painted in frost,
Mirrors of ice where car keys are lost.
A huddle of mittens, mismatched but warm,
A chilly surprise, but oh, so charming!

Pajama-clad kiddos sneak out to play,
Looking like marshmallows, all round and gray.
Tiny snowflakes, like giggles in flight,
Twist and turn in the morning light.

Slippers slide across frosty tiles,
Coffee's a battle; it takes a few tries.
Sticky fingers grab every toast slice,
Heading outside to roll like dice.

With cheeks red and noses aglow,
We sing carols for the snow to show.
The morning's a riddle, oh, what a jest,
Finding warmth in a frigid quest!

The Frosty Veil of Early Light

A blanket of white wraps every tree,
Squirrels in sweaters, oh, what a spree!
The whistle of tea kettles tunes the air,
While mittens fight battles without a care.

Sneaking outside, we tiptoe around,
Resisting the urge to fall to the ground.
Snowflakes glisten with a giggly cheer,
As my nephew declares, "This better not steer!"

Hot chocolate spills bring frights galore,
While marshmallows land, oh, what a score!
The dog's had a blast, frolicking fast,
But now he's a snowman, a frozen blast.

Let's gather and cheer, let invent some fun,
As day glimmers softly, the laughter's begun.
With frosty antics in frosty flights,
We'll claim sunny memories on chilly nights.

Paintings in Dim Slumber

In a world where teapots shiver,
Pajamas wear an icy thrill,
Snowflakes dance like disco balls,
Chillier than Aunt Edna's will.

Squirrels in hats, they plot and scheme,
Building forts with fluffy snow,
While penguins slide on ice cream streams,
Wishing they had hearts aglow.

Hot cocoa warms the frosty nights,
Marshmallows float like fluffy dreams,
But beware the llama in tights—
A chilly prank, or so it seems.

So here's to mornings dressed in chill,
Where laughter echoes like a bell,
With snowy socks and frosty thrills,
Spring, do come, and break this spell!

The Solstice's Frozen Portrait

Oh look at that snowman, what a sight,
With a carrot nose that doesn't quite fit,
He's posing for a portrait, oh what delight,
But those button eyes? They're just a bit lit!

Icicles dangle like wobbly teeth,
As snowflakes tease with a frosty fling,
Creating art that's sweet beneath,
A landscape where snowmen can only sing.

Winter's chill brings giggles and glee,
As mittens get lost on the frosty quest,
Rocking out with a hot cup of tea,
Skipping through snow, feeling quite blessed.

A world on ice, so oddly bright,
Where frosty giggles cover the ground,
So paint the canvas, hold on tight,
The solstice's smile is all around!

Time Capsules of the Cold

Beneath the frozen, twinkling cheer,
Lie memories wrapped in winter's hold,
A snowball fight, full of laughter and fear,
In time capsules, the stories unfold.

Eskimos in tiny teepees grin,
While polar bears throw snowball wars,
Frosty air is just the beginning,
Of winter's spirit that music adores.

Barrels of laughter, rolling down hills,
Until someone lands in a snowdrift deep,
Snowshoes squeaking, what merry thrills,
As secrets in frozen silence creep.

So gather 'round with cups of heat,
And share a tale, both funny and bold,
For winter's magic is quite a treat,
In time capsules, the cold can't withhold!

Light Beneath the Icy Veil

Under the shimmer of icy lace,
We tumble and twirl, a clumsy show,
Slides and slips, each a comical grace,
As frosty gales taunt, 'Come join the flow!'

Snow angels with sock puppets in flight,
Giggles erupt with each frosty dance,
Chasing shadows on a moonlit night,
When winter sprinkles her silly romance.

Even the owls seem to giggle and hoot,
As we bundle like marshmallows tight,
With frost-laden boots we stomp and tootle,
Creating chaos in wintry delight.

So let the chill work its merry cheer,
With laughter and warmth, we conquer each trail,
For underneath that icy veneer,
Lies a heart that's warm, beyond the pale!

A Mosaic of Shivers and Warmth

Beneath a blanket of fluffy white,
The kids slide down with giggles and might.
Hot cocoa spills as they dance and spin,
While snowmen wear scarves with cheeky grins.

Laughter echoes through the frosty air,
With mittens stuck in places quite rare.
The dog leaps high, a snowball in sight,
Chasing his tail is a hilarious sight!

Snowflakes twinkle like diamonds so bright,
Each one landing with a gentle light.
In this chilly world, together we play,
Wishing for summer to hurry one day!

But for now, we'll build, throw snow with glee,
In this wonderland, happy as can be.
With rosy cheeks, we'll vouch for the fun,
In a winter's embrace, we frolic and run.

The First Light's Icy Caress

The sun peeks out, yet the air's so brisk,
Sipping hot tea, oh, what a risky whisk!
I reached for a cup, but froze in my chair,
My fingers stuck, like they're saying 'don't dare!'

The ground is a blanket, untouched and white,
But in my slippers, I slip with a fright.
Falling in style, snowflakes all about,
How do they get me to giggle and shout?

Each morning's a treasure, a frosty surprise,
With breath visible like whispers and sighs.
The icicles dangle, like teeth of a beast,
As I glance outside, not ready for feast!

Yet somehow, behold! The fun wild and free,
Snowball fights waiting just outside with glee.
Let's laugh at the chill, and conquer the cold,
In each shivery moment, new stories unfold!

Beneath the Weight of a Pristine Sky

The trees wear white coats, a fashion so bold,
While squirrels dig deep for their breakfast of gold.
I shiver and laugh, hot chocolate spills,
As winter arrives with its tickling chills.

In boots that are fluffy and scarves worn askew,
It's a game of snowball—come join in the cue!
A launch and a giggle, oh so much fun,
Except when it lands with a splat on the run!

The sun's not so fierce, just peeking with care,
But snowflakes keep dancing, a gust in the air.
We never expect to slip—oh dear, there's a flop!
Rolling in laughter, we'll never just stop!

With cheeks rosy red, and smiles so wide,
We continue our game, let the hot chocolate glide.
Winter may shiver, but we twirl and we sway,
Embracing the chill, it's our favorite play!

Morning's Brush of Frosted Magic

When morning breaks with a chilly grin,
I dive in my blankets—please, let me win!
The toaster's reluctant; it pops out a thaw,
But my fingers squeal at the cold of the straw!

The windows are painted, ice art all around,
In boots all a-jingle, I slip on the ground.
Outside is a wonder, the world shines so bright,
It's madcap adventure, pure joy and delight!

With frosty eyebrows and snowflakes to catch,
I chuckle as I try a slippery batch.
A slip and a roll, and I'm down on the left,
But laughter is magic; I feel so adept!

With friends round to gather, in winter's embrace,
The battles of snowflakes bring smiles to each face.
So here's to the frosty, the fun, and the cheer,
In each frozen moment, we bring the warmth near!

Whispers of Winter's Breath

The air is crisp, a sneaky bite,
While squirrels debate in their nutty plight.
Snowflakes dance like they've lost their bets,
As snowmen nod, with no regrets.

Cups of cocoa in a frosty glow,
Sipping warmth while the cold winds blow.
Laughter echoes, a cheerful cheer,
As frostbite whispers, 'You'll regret that beer!'

Slippery paths bring a twisty dance,
Watch your step, or you might lose your pants!
Snowball fights unleash playful glee,
But snowballs packed too tight? That's the key!

In fluffy hats, we waddle with pride,
The chill in our cheeks, we cannot hide.
Winter's zany, a merry affair,
As snowflakes giggle in the frosty air.

Shimmering Silence of Dawn

Morning stretches, with a yawning sun,
The world in whispers, frozen fun.
Icicles hang like nature's teeth,
Chattering birds cling to their wreath.

Pancakes sizzle on the stovetop's edge,
While dogs in capes leap the snowy hedge.
Coffee brews with a frosty twist,
Mugs clink softly, like a wintry fist.

Neighbors bundled, as they complain,
About shoveling walks while freezing rain.
But smiles abound, like snowballs thrown,
Making the cold feel a little less known.

Chasing the dawn with cotton-candied skies,
Frolicking laughter, as cold-breath flies.
Frosty fingers, yet spirits high,
A twist of winter, support the sly.

Crystal Dreams on Icy Shores

Waves of frost dance on silent ground,
While snowflakes swirl without a sound.
A penguin struts in the frozen breeze,
Trying to impress, but just can't tease.

Seagulls in sweaters, a sight bizarre,
Debating fish, who's more bizarre.
An ice-cream cone that's frozen hard,
As kids giggle at their frosty yard.

Snowmen build a fort with flair,
But carrot noses go flying through the air!
Toboggan slides, a fun-filled race,
But watch for trees; they're never misplaced!

Crystal dreams in a sea of light,
Wrapped in laughter, oh, what a sight!
Winter wraps us, like a giant hug,
With giggles chasing, a joyous rug.

Chasing Shadows in Silver Light

At dusk we chase those shadows long,
With light so soft, it feels like a song.
Snow angels giggle as they drape,
While coats of wool muffle our escape.

The sky blushes in hues of blue,
As laughter rings out, a joyful crew.
Snowflakes land, a sparkling surprise,
We catch them all, just like butterflies.

Icicles dangle like hesitant toes,
Our frosty breaths form clouds, like prose.
Around the fire, we spin our tales,
Of epic sled rides and winter gales.

Chasing shadows, we leap and spin,
In the magic of cold, let the fun begin!
Winter's mischief in laughter will bright,
As we dance away under silver light.

The Silence of Winter's Breath

Chilly air with a tinge of white,
Socks on my hands feels just right.
The snowman stands, looking quite grand,
But I can't feel my toes in this land.

Birds in jackets, all snug and tight,
They chirp about, what a silly sight!
I slipped on ice, oh what a scene,
Like I'm in a cartoon, I must lean.

Coffee's cold, but that's no crime,
It can wait, I'm having a time!
The cat's in boots, all happy and spry,
Chasing after snowflakes, oh so sly!

Winter's here, but who needs a hat?
I have my scarf tied, looking like a brat.
With all this chill, I dance with glee,
Who knew cold could be so free?

A Symphony of Snowflakes

Tiny dancers from the sky,
Land on my nose, oh my oh my!
In their twirls, they laugh and play,
Who knew winter was a cabaret?

Snowballs fly, oh what a blast,
But my aim's poor, I run quite fast.
The dog joins in, it's all a game,
He wears my glove, we share the fame!

Hot cocoa spills, a chocolaty mess,
I tried to stir, but caused distress.
While sipping warm, I giggle and grin,
Who needs a mug? I'll drink from the tin!

Snowflakes bow and then depart,
Leaving their magic in every heart.
Winter plays a funny tune,
With giggles rising, oh how we swoon!

Shimmering Veil of Hibernation

Naps are long, what bliss this brings,
Pajamas on, and happy things.
Outside the world is white and bright,
Inside my blanket, I'm out of sight.

Squirrels wintering, plump and stout,
They're living large, while I pout.
I found a doughnut under the chair,
It's a treasure, a sweet affair!

Froze my last slice of pizza too,
A winter twist, who knew it's true?
I'll test the fridge on a chilly day,
Hoping for magic or a gourmet tray!

As I cozy up, views become grand,
Painting frosty dreams, not all planned.
So here's to slumbers in frozen bliss,
In this veil, I find my happy twist!

Morning's Chilling Embrace

Alarm rings loud, I hit snooze twice,
Huddled in blankets, oh how nice!
The world waits outside with frosty shrouds,
While I enjoy my cozy clouds.

Teeth chattering like a castanets' play,
But I refuse to start my day!
Coffee brews like a wizard's spell,
Still in pajama heaven, feel so well.

Nature's got the cold maxed out,
Ducks are waddling, have no doubt.
I laugh at those bold, braving the chill,
With hot chocolate dreams, I'm rolling still!

As sunshine teases through icy trees,
I slip into warmth, with utmost ease.
Mornings are silly, with laughter and cheer,
Winter hugs tightly, "Stay close, my dear!"

The Wisp of a Faint Sun

A flicker of warmth in a sea of blue,
The snowmen look puzzled, with nothing to do.
Their carrots are drooping, their smiles have froze,
While squirrels in thick jackets discuss winter's prose.

The whispers of morning with a comedic twirl,
A snowball fight starts, giving each dog a whirl.
The sun peeks in cautiously, tickling our cheeks,
As snowflakes play tag like mischievous freaks.

With snow on our boots and laughter in tow,
We dance in the drifts, letting our troubles go.
Oh what a sight, with the neighbor's old cat,
As it slips on the ice—now that's where it's at!

So here's to the mornings when frost bites our toes,
When humor shines bright, and the silliness flows.
We'll toast to the chill with a hot cup of cheer,
And laugh at the chaos that keeps winter near!

Hushed Secrets in Crystalline Snow

The trees are all dressed up in white fluffy gowns,
While icicles dangle like cold frowny clowns.
A snow angel tries to escape wiggly arms,
Oh, the giggles abound as it lacks all its charms!

A whisper goes round through the frostbitten air,
The owls roll their eyes, setting up a fair.
The snowflakes do pirouettes, not caring for grace,
As rabbits hop by with a worrisome face.

Each step on the path makes a delightful crunch,
As belly laughs echo, bringing winter a bunch.
Muffin-topped neighbors chase their big, fluffy hounds,
While snowballs are thrown—who knew chaos abounds?

So let's grab our mittens and strut out the door,
To make some bad snowmen, then ask for encore.
We'll scheme with the frost, under skies so absurd,
And cherish the secrets that can't be disturbed!

The Quietude Before the Bloom

A soft hush descends as the snowflakes lay thick,
We ponder a snow day—should we sled or stick?
With marshmallows floating in cocoa so warm,
Winter's comedic pause keeps us safe from harm.

The garden lies dormant, a snooze in the frost,
Yet squirrels in pajamas have determined the cost.
They bumble and fumble in frantic delight,
Snatching up acorns as they scamper in flight.

The moments of stillness have a silly side,
As snowmen hold hands like a whimsical ride.
The crispy cold air laced with giggle-filled sighs,
Winter's pure humor reflected in our eyes.

So let's catch the quiet, let it fill us with glee,
As we tiptoe through snow, filled with joy and esprit.
Let's cherish the laughter beneath frosty dreams,
And wait for the blooms in the sunlight's warm beams!

An Invitation to Icy Pastures

Come join in the mischief, the snowflakes invite,
To frolic and stumble, make memories bright.
In fields cold and fluffy, where nobody's seen,
The footprints we leave are the best kind of sheen.

With hot chocolate mustaches and sleigh rides so fine,
We'll play in the drifts till the stars start to shine.
The moon is a smile, watching all from its height,
While penguins on skates bring all our joy to light.

So grab your warm scarf and your most wobbly hat,
Let's build an odd creature—oh, what do you think that?
With mismatched parts, it'll surely take flight,
An icy creation, pure wacky delight!

An invitation spread, all around in a swirl,
To laugh with the snowflakes and give them a twirl.
So come one, come all, to this wintery space,
Where humor runs wild in a cuddly embrace!